HOW TO NEGOTIATE YOUR SALARY AND BENEFITS

The Essential Guide to Advocating for Your Worth and Maximizing Compensation

Jordan Motivator

TABLE OF CONTENT

INTRODUCTION

Did you know that negotiating a higher salary can substantially impact your lifetime earnings? In fact, studies show that a well-negotiated salary increase can add over half a million dollars to your overall income trajectory. Imagine the doors that could open, the investments you could make, and the financial security you could attain by harnessing the power of negotiation. Your ability to negotiate is not just a soft skill; it's a direct contributor to your financial well-being.

Yet, despite the undeniable impact, many individuals find themselves paralyzed by common fears and struggles when it comes to negotiating. The lack of confidence, anxiety about rocking the boat, and the uncertainty of what to ask for or how much one is truly worth can be daunting obstacles. The cost of not negotiating, however, is even more significant. It's not just about leaving money on the table; it's about missing out on the financial rewards and benefits that should rightfully be yours.

This book is your key to overcoming these challenges and unlocking the full potential of your compensation. It offers proven strategies, practical scripts, and a roadmap to master negotiation in the realm of salaries and benefits. From researching reasonable salaries to building unwavering confidence, making a compelling pitch to responding adeptly to counteroffers, and navigating the intricacies of negotiating benefits, this guide covers every facet of the negotiation process. It is a comprehensive resource designed to empower you with the knowledge and skills needed to secure the pay and benefits you deserve.

Allow me to illustrate the transformative power of these negotiation approaches through a real-life example. Meet Jane, who, by applying the strategies outlined in this book, not only gained the confidence to negotiate her salary but also increased her earnings significantly, propelling her career to new heights. Her story serves as a testament to the effectiveness of the techniques you're about to learn.

It's time to take charge of your financial future right now. Dive into the pages ahead, absorb the wisdom within, and embark on a journey towards not just a job, but a thriving career. It's time to leverage the advice provided here and confidently negotiate the pay and benefits you rightfully deserve. The financial upside awaits those who take action – and that someone could very well be you.

Why Negotiating Salary and Benefits is Important

Negotiating salary and benefits is a critical and empowering step in the professional journey, holding far-reaching implications for both immediate financial well-being and long-term career satisfaction. Understanding the importance of this process goes beyond the desire for increased earnings; it is about recognizing and asserting the value you bring to an organization.

Maximizing Your Earning Potential:

Negotiating salary is a direct means of ensuring that your compensation aligns with the value of your skills, experience, and contributions. Accepting an initial offer without negotiation may mean leaving money on the table, hindering your ability to build wealth, save for the future, and achieve financial goals.

Reflecting Your Market Value:

The job market is dynamic, with salary standards evolving based on industry trends and demand for specific skills. Negotiating allows you to stay current and reflect your true market value. This ensures that you are compensated in line with industry benchmarks, acknowledging the unique expertise you bring to the table.

Career Satisfaction and Motivation:

Recognizing and advocating for your worth contributes to a sense of professional validation. When your compensation reflects your contributions, job satisfaction increases, leading to heightened motivation and engagement. This, in turn, positively impacts your overall performance and career trajectory.

Building Financial Security:

Negotiating salary and benefits isn't just about immediate financial gains; it's a strategic move toward long-term financial security. A well-negotiated compensation package can impact retirement savings, investments, and the ability to weather unexpected financial challenges, providing a foundation for a more stable future.

Setting a Baseline for Future Earnings:

The salary negotiated at the outset of a job often serves as the baseline for future raises and advancements. Negotiating a competitive starting salary establishes a foundation for ongoing career growth, ensuring that subsequent raises build upon a solid financial base.

Valuing Your Unique Contributions:

Beyond monetary considerations, negotiating benefits allows you to shape a comprehensive compensation package that values your individual needs and priorities. This may include healthcare benefits, flexible work arrangements, professional development opportunities, and more, contributing to a well-rounded and fulfilling work experience.

Empowering Equal Pay:

Negotiating salary is a crucial element in addressing gender and diversity gaps in pay. By advocating for fair and equitable compensation, individuals contribute to the broader societal goal of achieving equal pay for equal work, fostering a more inclusive and just workforce.

In essence, negotiating salary and benefits is not just a transactional aspect of employment; it is a strategic investment in your professional worth and future success. It is an assertion of your value, a pathway to financial security, and a demonstration of your commitment to fostering a rewarding and mutually beneficial professional relationship.

Overcoming Common Hesitations

Negotiating salary and benefits can be a daunting task, often accompanied by common hesitations that may hold individuals back from asserting their true worth. Understanding and overcoming these reservations is a crucial step toward realizing your full earning potential and securing a compensation package that aligns with your value. Here are some of the most common hesitations and strategies to conquer them:

Lack of Confidence:

Hesitation: Many individuals feel a lack of confidence when approaching the negotiation table, fearing that they may come across as too assertive or demanding.

Strategy: Build confidence by thoroughly researching industry salary standards and preparing a comprehensive list of your accomplishments and skills. Practice your negotiation pitch with a trusted friend or mentor to refine your delivery and boost your self-assurance.

Fear of Rejection or Confrontation:

Hesitation: The fear of facing rejection or creating an uncomfortable situation can deter individuals from negotiating.

Strategy: Approach negotiation as a collaborative conversation rather than a confrontation. Emphasize the mutual benefit of reaching a fair agreement. Rehearse responses to potential objections to feel more prepared and in control, reducing the fear of rejection.

Uncertainty About Market Value:

Hesitation: Not knowing one's true market value can lead to hesitations in negotiating, as individuals may be unsure about what constitutes a reasonable request.

Strategy: Conduct thorough research on industry salary benchmarks, taking into account your experience, skills, and geographical location. Leverage online resources, salary surveys, and networking to gain a comprehensive understanding of your market value.

Fear of Damaging the Relationship:

Hesitation: Individuals may worry that negotiating could strain the employer-employee relationship, potentially affecting future opportunities and collaboration.

Strategy: Approach negotiation professionally and diplomatically, emphasizing your commitment to contributing to the organization's success. Frame your requests in a positive light, focusing on the value you bring and your shared goals.

Not Knowing What to Ask For:

Hesitation: The lack of clarity on what to ask for, whether in terms of salary figures or additional benefits, can create hesitations in initiating negotiations.

Strategy: Prioritize your needs and desires, considering both financial and non-financial aspects. Research common benefits within your industry and prepare a range for your salary expectations. Be specific about your requirements to facilitate a more constructive negotiation.

Underestimating Personal Value:

Hesitation: Some individuals may downplay their accomplishments and contributions, leading to a reluctance to assert their true value.

Strategy: Create a detailed list of your achievements, skills, and unique contributions to the organization. Recognize your worth and articulate it confidently during negotiations. Seek external feedback from mentors or colleagues to gain a more objective perspective on your value.

By acknowledging and addressing these common hesitations, individuals can embark on the negotiation process with greater confidence and strategic clarity. Negotiation is not just about seeking personal gain; it is a collaborative effort to establish a fair and mutually beneficial professional relationship. Overcoming these hesitations is a vital step toward realizing the full potential of your compensation package.

Researching Salaries And Benefits

Before entering negotiations, a crucial step is conducting thorough research on salaries and benefits within your industry and geographic location. This process empowers you with valuable insights, allowing you to establish a well-informed and reasonable foundation for your compensation expectations. Here's a strategic guide to researching salaries and benefits:

Utilizing Online Resources:

Salary Websites: Explore dedicated salary websites such as Glassdoor, PayScale, and Salary.com. These platforms provide crowdsourced data, allowing you to compare salaries for specific roles in various industries.

Company Reviews: In addition to salary information, read company reviews on platforms like Glassdoor to gain insights into the overall compensation packages and workplace cultures of potential employers.

Networking for Insider Insights:

Professional Associations: Connect with professional associations related to your industry. Attend networking events, conferences, or webinars to gather insights on prevailing salary standards and benefit trends.

Industry Peers: Engage in conversations with current or former colleagues, mentors, or industry peers to gain firsthand knowledge about compensation practices. Insights from those with similar roles can be particularly valuable.

Consulting Recruitment Agencies:

Recruitment Professionals: Reach out to recruitment agencies specializing in your field. Professionals in these agencies often have extensive knowledge of salary ranges and benefit structures within specific industries and can provide tailored advice based on your skills and experience.

Understanding Regional Variances:

Cost of Living Adjustments: Consider regional cost-of-living variations when researching salaries. Salaries in high-cost cities may be higher to offset living expenses. Tools like cost-of-living calculators can help you adjust expectations based on your location.

Analyzing Comprehensive Benefits:

Health and Wellness Programs: Research the health and wellness benefits offered by companies. Evaluate healthcare coverage, wellness programs, and any additional perks related to employee well-being.

Retirement Plans and Stock Options: Understand the retirement plans and stock options provided. Analyze the employer's contributions to retirement savings and the availability of stock-based compensation, if applicable.

Considering Non-Monetary Benefits:

Flexible Work Arrangements: Investigate the availability of flexible work arrangements, including remote work options and flexible hours.

Professional Development Opportunities: Assess opportunities for professional growth, including training programs, educational support, and career advancement prospects.

Evaluating Total Compensation Packages:

Bonus Structures: Explore bonus structures within the industry. Understand how performance bonuses are typically determined and awarded.

Total Compensation Calculators: Some companies provide total compensation calculators that estimate the overall value of your package, including salary, bonuses, benefits, and perks.

Remember, accurate and up-to-date research forms the foundation for a successful negotiation. Armed with a comprehensive understanding of industry standards and company practices, you can confidently articulate your value and negotiate a compensation package that aligns with your skills and contributions.

Understanding Your Value

In the realm of career negotiations, understanding your own value is not just a self-affirming exercise; it is a strategic imperative that shapes the trajectory of your professional journey. Recognizing the unique blend of skills, experiences, and contributions you bring to the table is fundamental to effectively conveying your worth to potential employers. Here's a guide to unlocking the power of understanding your value:

Self-Reflection and Assessment:

Skills Inventory: Conduct a comprehensive inventory of your skills, both technical and soft. Identify the skills that set you apart and contribute to your effectiveness in your current or desired role.

Achievements and Accomplishments: Reflect on your past achievements and accomplishments. What projects have you excelled in? How have you positively impacted your team or organization?

Quantifying Contributions:

Tangible Results: Translate your contributions into quantifiable results. Whether it's revenue growth, cost savings, or process improvements, quantifying your impact provides concrete evidence of your value.

Metrics and KPIs: Familiarize yourself with key performance indicators (KPIs) relevant to your role. Align your achievements with these metrics to demonstrate your effectiveness in measurable terms.

Benchmarking Against Industry Standards:

Industry Research: Understand the industry benchmarks for your role. Compare your skills, experiences, and achievements against the standards prevalent in your sector. This contextualizes your value within the broader professional landscape.

Salary Research: While researching salaries, take note of the typical compensation for professionals with similar qualifications and experience. This information not only guides your salary expectations but also reinforces the value placed on your expertise.

Seeking Feedback:

Professional Network: Solicit feedback from your professional network, including colleagues, mentors, and industry peers. External perspectives can provide valuable insights into your strengths and areas for further development.

Performance Reviews: Reflect on feedback received during performance reviews. Identify recurring themes or areas where your contributions have been particularly noteworthy.

Continuous Learning and Skill Development:

Professional Development Plans: Demonstrate your commitment to growth by actively engaging in continuous learning. Showcase your dedication to staying updated on industry trends and acquiring new skills that enhance your overall value.

Certifications and Training: Highlight relevant certifications and training programs completed. These credentials reinforce your expertise and underscore your commitment to professional development.

Effective Communication:

Elevator Pitch: Develop a concise and compelling elevator pitch that encapsulates your value proposition. This succinct summary should articulate who you are, what you bring to the table, and the impact you've had in your career.

Storytelling: Narrate your professional journey through storytelling. Share anecdotes that illustrate your problem-solving abilities, leadership skills, and resilience. A well-crafted narrative enhances the understanding of your value.

Understanding your value is not a static process but a dynamic journey of self-discovery and growth. By mastering this awareness, you not only fortify your position in negotiations but also cultivate a deepened sense of professional identity. Armed with a comprehensive understanding of your worth, you step into negotiations with the confidence and clarity necessary to secure a compensation package that reflects your true value.

Setting Goals For Negotiation

Setting clear and strategic goals is a fundamental prelude to any successful negotiation. Whether you're aiming to secure a competitive salary, enhanced benefits, or a combination of both, establishing well-defined objectives is essential to guide your negotiation process. Here's a guide to help you set goals for negotiation effectively:

Define Your Priorities:

Financial Objectives: Clearly outline your financial goals, including the desired salary, bonuses, and any specific monetary perks. Consider your current financial situation, industry standards, and the value you bring to the role.

Non-Monetary Priorities: Identify non-monetary aspects that are crucial for your job satisfaction. This could include flexible work hours, remote work options, professional development opportunities, or unique benefits tailored to your needs.

Research Industry Standards:

Salary Benchmarks: Ground your goals in industry benchmarks by researching the typical compensation for your role and experience level.

This ensures that your financial expectations align with prevailing standards, strengthening your negotiation position.

Benefit Comparisons: Investigate the benefits commonly offered within your industry. Understanding the standard benefits package helps you articulate reasonable requests and negotiate effectively.

Consider Your Value Proposition:

Quantifiable Contributions: Align your goals with your quantifiable contributions to the organization. If you've consistently achieved goals, increased efficiency, or contributed to revenue growth, leverage these achievements to support your compensation requests.

Long-Term Impact: Factor in the long-term impact of your role on the organization. If your responsibilities contribute to strategic objectives, emphasize this when setting goals to underscore your importance within the company.

Establish a Realistic Range:

Minimum Acceptable Offer: Determine the minimum compensation package you find acceptable. This acts as a baseline and ensures you don't accept an offer that falls below your needs or market value.

Aspirational Goals: Set aspirational goals that reflect your ideal scenario. While ambitious, these goals provide room for negotiation and allow for potential concessions during the process.

Balance Assertiveness with Flexibility:

Assertive Communication: Cultivate assertive communication skills to clearly express your goals without ambiguity. Be confident in articulating the value you bring and why you deserve the proposed package.

Flexibility in Negotiation: Acknowledge that negotiations involve a give-and-take. Be open to alternative proposals and demonstrate flexibility while maintaining focus on achieving your core goals.

Anticipate and Prepare for Counteroffers:

Counteroffer Strategies: Anticipate potential counteroffers and establish strategies to respond effectively. Know your priorities and areas where you can compromise, ensuring you're prepared for various negotiation scenarios.

Balancing Trade-Offs: Understand the trade-offs you are willing to make. This may involve adjusting salary expectations in exchange for increased benefits or vice versa.

Timeline and Milestones:

Set Negotiation Timeline: Establish a realistic timeline for the negotiation process. Consider key milestones, such as when to initiate discussions, respond to offers, and finalize agreements.

Prepare for Incremental Progress: Recognize that negotiations may unfold gradually. Set interim goals and milestones to gauge progress and make adjustments as needed.

By setting clear, well-researched goals for negotiation, you position yourself as a informed and strategic professional. These goals serve as a roadmap, guiding your interactions and ensuring that the final agreement aligns with your professional aspirations and financial expectations.

Strengthening Your Position

Negotiating effectively requires more than just setting goals; it involves actively strengthening your position to ensure a favorable outcome. Here's a comprehensive guide on how to fortify your stance and navigate negotiations with confidence:

Leverage Your Unique Value Proposition:

Highlight Achievements: Emphasize specific accomplishments and contributions that set you apart. Showcase how your skills and achievements align with the company's goals and needs.

Quantify Impact: Use quantifiable metrics to illustrate the tangible impact of your work. Whether it's revenue growth, cost savings, or process improvements, quantifying your contributions adds weight to your value proposition.

Demonstrate Market Knowledge:

Industry Insights: Showcase your understanding of industry trends, market benchmarks, and the competitive landscape. This demonstrates that your salary expectations are grounded in the current market value for your role.

Competitor Analysis: If applicable, reference compensation practices at competitor organizations to highlight your awareness of prevailing industry standards.

Emphasize Specialized Skills and Expertise:

Niche Skills: If you possess specialized skills or certifications, underscore their relevance to the role and how they contribute to the organization's success.

Unique Expertise: Articulate how your unique expertise addresses specific challenges within the company, making you an invaluable asset.

Position Yourself as an Investment:

Future Contributions: Emphasize your potential for future growth within the company. Present yourself as an investment that will yield long-term returns through sustained contributions.

Alignment with Company Goals: Demonstrate how your goals align with the company's strategic objectives, reinforcing your commitment to its success.

Build on Positive Relationships:

Network Within the Company: If you have internal contacts, discreetly gather information about the company's negotiation culture and practices. Positive relationships can provide insights and endorsements.

Professional References: If applicable, use positive references or testimonials from colleagues, supervisors, or clients to bolster your professional reputation.

Anticipate and Address Concerns:

Proactively Address Weaknesses: Identify potential concerns the employer might have and address them proactively. This could include addressing gaps in experience or providing plans for skill development.

Mitigate Perceived Risks: If there are perceived risks associated with your candidacy, offer solutions or assurances that mitigate those concerns.

Flexible but Strategic Concessions:

Prioritize Non-Monetary Benefits: If monetary negotiations reach an impasse, emphasize the importance of non-monetary benefits. This flexibility showcases your willingness to find mutually beneficial solutions.

Highlight Trade-Offs: When making concessions, strategically highlight the value you're giving up while signaling the importance of receiving comparable value in return.

Embrace Collaborative Language:

Team Player Mentality: Use collaborative language to convey that you are a team player. Highlight instances where your collaboration has positively impacted projects and emphasize your commitment to the team's success.

Win-Win Solutions: Position the negotiation as an opportunity for a win-win outcome, where both parties can derive value and satisfaction.

Maintain Professionalism and Confidence:

Professional Demeanor: Throughout the negotiation, maintain a professional and positive demeanor. Avoid confrontational language and focus on a collaborative approach.

Confident Communication: Speak confidently about your value, contributions, and expectations. Assertive but respectful communication enhances your credibility.

Be Prepared to Walk Away:

Know Your Limits: Establish clear boundaries and know your minimum acceptable offer. Being prepared to walk away signals to the employer that you are serious about your value and have alternatives.

Explore Other Opportunities: If negotiations become challenging, explore alternative job opportunities to strengthen your negotiating position.

By strategically implementing these tactics, you not only fortify your position but also create a compelling narrative about your value and contributions. A well-prepared and confident negotiation strategy significantly increases the likelihood of achieving a favorable outcome aligned with your goals.

Effective Communication Tips

Effective communication is the cornerstone of successful negotiations. Whether you are discussing salary, benefits, or other terms, how you convey your thoughts and needs can significantly impact the outcome. Here are key tips to enhance your communication skills during negotiations:

Active Listening:

Focus on Understanding: Pay close attention to what the other party is saying. Avoid formulating your response while they speak. Understanding their perspective is crucial for finding common ground.

Clarity and Conciseness:

Clear and Direct Language: Express your thoughts clearly and directly. Avoid ambiguous or overly complex language. Clarity fosters a better understanding of your position and expectations.

Confidence and Poise:

Maintain Composure: Project confidence through your body language, tone, and choice of words. Maintain eye contact and a composed demeanor. Confidence reinforces the credibility of your arguments.

Empathy:

Understand Their Perspective: Put yourself in the other party's shoes. Understanding their motivations and concerns allows you to tailor your communication to resonate with their needs.

Positivity and Collaboration:

Use Positive Language: Frame your statements positively. Instead of saying "I can't accept that," consider expressing, "I was hoping for...". This fosters a collaborative atmosphere rather than a confrontational one.

Ask Open-Ended Questions:

Encourage Dialogue: Pose open-ended questions to encourage the other party to share more information. This not only demonstrates interest but also provides valuable insights for crafting mutually beneficial solutions.

Non-Verbal Communication:

Body Language: Be mindful of your body language. Maintain an open posture, avoid crossing arms, and use gestures to emphasize points. Sincerity and confidence can be communicated by nonverbal signs.

Use of Silence:

Strategic Pauses: Embrace strategic pauses during the conversation. Silence can be a powerful tool, allowing the other party time to consider your points and respond thoughtfully.

Stay Calm and Flexible:

Adaptability: Be prepared to adapt to unexpected turns in the conversation. Staying calm under pressure demonstrates your ability to handle challenges and contributes to a constructive negotiation environment.

Avoid Assumptions:

Seek Clarification: If something is unclear, ask for clarification rather than making assumptions. Misunderstandings can be costly, and seeking clarification demonstrates your commitment to clear communication.

Respectful Tone:

Maintain Professionalism: Keep the tone of the conversation respectful and professional. Don't shout at people or use rude words. Professionalism enhances the likelihood of a positive outcome.

Summarize and Confirm:

Recap Key Points: Periodically summarize key points to ensure mutual understanding. Confirming agreement on specific details prevents misunderstandings and reinforces your commitment to transparency.

Express Gratitude:

Thank Them for Their Time: Regardless of the negotiation's outcome, express gratitude for their time and willingness to engage in the discussion. A positive closing note leaves the door open for future collaboration.

Remember, effective communication is a dynamic skill that evolves with practice. By incorporating these tips into your negotiation strategy, you can create a communication framework that fosters understanding, collaboration, and ultimately, success in achieving your negotiation goals.

Presenting Your Case Persuasively

Presenting your case persuasively is a crucial skill in negotiations, as it can significantly influence the outcome of discussions related to salary, benefits, or other terms. Here are key strategies to enhance the persuasiveness of your case:

Craft a Compelling Narrative:

Storytelling: Frame your case as a compelling narrative. Share anecdotes that highlight your achievements, challenges overcome, and the positive impact of your contributions. A well-told story engages and resonates with your audience.

Quantify Your Contributions:

Use Metrics: Quantify your achievements wherever possible. Whether it's revenue growth, cost savings, or project success, using concrete metrics adds credibility to your claims and reinforces the tangible value you bring.

Align with Company Objectives:

Show Alignment: Clearly demonstrate how your goals and contributions align with the company's strategic objectives. Illustrate how your success contributes to the organization's overall success.

Highlight Unique Value Proposition:

Emphasize Uniqueness: Clearly articulate what sets you apart from others. Highlight unique skills, experiences, or qualities that make you an invaluable asset to the team or organization.

Address Pain Points:

Solve Problems: Identify and address potential pain points or challenges the company is facing. Position yourself as a solution to these challenges, emphasizing your ability to contribute positively.

Utilize Visuals:

Charts and Graphs: If applicable, use visual aids such as charts or graphs to illustrate your points.

Visual representations can simplify complex information and make your case more memorable.

Anticipate and Address Concerns:

Proactive Solutions: Anticipate potential concerns the other party may have and proactively provide solutions. Demonstrating foresight and problem-solving skills strengthens your case.

Show Growth and Development:

Highlight Progress: Showcase your professional growth and development over time. Emphasize how your skills have evolved, contributing to your current capabilities and readiness for new challenges.

Use Strong, Positive Language:

Confident Expression: Use assertive and positive language to express your points. Phrases like "I have consistently demonstrated..." convey confidence and certainty in your abilities.

Refer to Market Value:

Industry Benchmarks: Reference industry benchmarks and standards when discussing compensation. Highlighting your awareness of market value strengthens your position and sets realistic expectations.

Demonstrate Flexibility:

Concessions with Purpose: If necessary, demonstrate flexibility by offering concessions strategically. This shows a willingness to collaborate and find mutually beneficial solutions.

Emphasize Team Contribution:

Team Player Mentality: Highlight instances where your contributions have positively impacted team dynamics or collaborative projects. Emphasizing your ability to work seamlessly within a team reinforces your value.

Reinforce Future Potential:

Growth Opportunities: Discuss your aspirations and how your continued growth within the company will contribute to its success. Reinforce that investing in your development is an investment in the organization's future.

Practice and Refine:

Rehearse Your Pitch: Practice presenting your case beforehand. This helps you refine your message, ensures clarity, and enhances your delivery during the actual negotiation.

Remain Open to Collaboration:

Collaborative Language: Frame your case in a way that invites collaboration. Use language that emphasizes finding common ground and working together to achieve shared goals.

By combining these strategies, you can present your case in a persuasive and compelling manner, increasing the likelihood of achieving your negotiation objectives. Remember to be confident, adaptable, and focused on building a mutually beneficial agreement.

Responding To Counteroffers

Receiving a counteroffer during negotiations is a common and pivotal moment in the process. How you respond to a counteroffer can shape the trajectory of the negotiation and influence the final outcome. Here's a strategic guide on effectively responding to counteroffers:

Express Appreciation:

Gratitude: Begin your response by expressing gratitude for the counteroffer. Acknowledge the effort put into crafting an alternative and convey your appreciation for the ongoing dialogue.

Take Time to Evaluate:

Request for Time: Politely request some time to carefully evaluate the counteroffer. This gives you the opportunity to analyze the terms, consider your priorities, and formulate a thoughtful response.

Assess Alignment with Goals:

Review Goals: Revisit your initial goals and priorities. Assess how the counteroffer aligns with your objectives, both in terms of compensation and other aspects such as benefits, work-life balance, and professional development.

Points of Agreement:

Highlight Common Ground: Identify areas of agreement between your initial proposal and the counteroffer. This sets a positive tone and emphasizes the shared interests that form the basis for a successful negotiation.

Clarify Ambiguities:

Seek Clarification: If any aspects of the counteroffer are unclear, seek clarification. It's essential to have a complete understanding of the terms and conditions before proceeding further.

Reiterate Your Value:

Emphasize Your Worth: Remind the employer of your unique value proposition and contributions. Reinforce why you are a valuable asset to the organization, linking your skills and experiences to their business needs.

Articulate Concerns Professionally:

Address Concerns: If there are specific aspects of the counteroffer that concern you, articulate them professionally. Use diplomatic language to express your reservations and provide context for your perspective.

Offer Constructive Feedback:

Suggest Alternatives: If there are elements of the counteroffer that are challenging for you, offer constructive alternatives. Propose creative solutions that could meet both parties' needs, fostering a collaborative negotiation atmosphere.

Consider the Entire Package:

Holistic Evaluation: Evaluate the entire compensation package, including non-monetary benefits. Sometimes, a counteroffer may include adjustments to benefits or other perks that contribute to the overall value.

Revisit Your Bottom Line:

Clarify Minimum Acceptance: If the counteroffer is not fully aligned with your expectations, be prepared to clarify your minimum acceptable terms. Communicate your bottom line while remaining open to finding middle ground.

Maintain Professionalism:

Professional Tone: Keep your response professional and composed. Avoid a confrontational or adversarial tone, and instead, focus on maintaining a positive and collaborative dialogue.

Indicate Willingness to Negotiate:

Express Openness: Communicate your continued willingness to negotiate. Emphasize that you are committed to finding a mutually beneficial agreement and that the negotiation process is an opportunity for collaboration.

Reaffirm Commitment:

Reiterate Interest: Reaffirm your interest in the position and the organization. Reassure the employer that your goal is to reach a fair and mutually satisfying agreement that aligns with both parties' interests.

Seek Face-to-Face Discussion:

Request a Meeting: If the negotiation process allows, consider proposing a face-to-face or virtual meeting. Direct communication can facilitate a more nuanced discussion and help build a stronger rapport.

Evaluate Long-Term Implications:

Consider Long-Term Impact: Assess the long-term implications of your response. Strive for a resolution that not only meets your immediate needs but also sets a positive tone for your future relationship with the employer.

Responding to counteroffers is a delicate dance that requires a combination of strategic thinking, effective communication, and a focus on mutual benefits. By approaching counteroffers with a thoughtful and collaborative mindset, you increase the likelihood of reaching a satisfying agreement for both parties.

Staying Poised Under Pressure

Negotiations, especially those involving salary and benefits, can be high-stakes and emotionally charged. Maintaining composure under pressure is essential for effective communication and decision-making. Here are strategies to help you stay poised during negotiations:

Prioritize Preparation:

Thorough Research: Prioritize comprehensive preparation before entering negotiations. Thoroughly research industry standards, company practices, and your own value proposition. Being well-prepared builds confidence.

Set Realistic Expectations:

Define Realistic Goals: Set realistic and achievable goals for the negotiation. Having a clear understanding of what you realistically expect helps manage expectations and reduces pressure.

Breathe and Center Yourself:

Deep Breaths: When feeling pressure rising, take deep, calming breaths. Center yourself by focusing on your breath to regain mental clarity and control over your emotions.

Positive Self-Talk:

Affirmations: Use positive self-talk to reinforce your confidence. Remind yourself of your achievements, skills, and the value you bring to the table. Positive affirmations can bolster your mindset.

Focus on the Long-Term:

Big Picture Perspective: Shift your focus from immediate stress to the long-term goals. Remind yourself that negotiations are part of a broader career journey, and maintaining professionalism pays off in the long run.

Anticipate Challenges:

Mental Rehearsal: Anticipate potential challenges or objections and mentally rehearse your responses. This proactive approach helps you feel more prepared to handle unexpected turns in the negotiation.

Establish Communication Breaks:

Pause Strategically: If emotions are escalating, establish moments during the negotiation to take a brief break. A strategic pause allows you to collect your thoughts and respond more thoughtfully.

Focus on Solutions, Not Just Problems:

Problem-Solving Mindset: Adopt a mindset that focuses on finding solutions rather than dwelling on problems. This proactive approach helps shift the energy in the negotiation towards collaboration.

Adopt a Neutral Tone:

Maintain Neutral Language: Use neutral and professional language throughout the negotiation. Avoid confrontational or defensive tones, as they can escalate tension.

Practice Active Listening:

Stay Present: Actively listen to the other party's concerns and perspectives. Being present in the moment helps you better understand their position and respond appropriately.

Visualize Success:

Positive Visualization: Visualize a successful negotiation outcome. Picture yourself confidently articulating your points and reaching a mutually beneficial agreement. Positive visualization can influence your actual performance.

Acknowledge Emotions, Don't React Impulsively:

Emotional Awareness: Acknowledge your emotions without immediately reacting. If you feel frustration or stress building, take a moment to process before responding. This self-awareness prevents impulsive reactions.

Use Humor Appropriately:

Lighten the Atmosphere: Appropriately using humor can diffuse tension and lighten the atmosphere. Be mindful of the context and ensure your humor is inclusive and non-confrontational.

Stay Flexible in Approach:

Adaptability: Be open to adapting your approach based on the flow of the negotiation. Flexibility allows you to respond to changing dynamics without feeling overwhelmed.

Reflect and Learn:

Post-Negotiation Reflection: After the negotiation, take time to reflect on your performance. Identify areas for improvement and celebrate successes. Learning from each experience contributes to your growth under pressure.

Remember, staying poised under pressure is a skill that develops with practice. By integrating these strategies into your negotiation toolkit, you not only enhance your ability to navigate challenging discussions but also contribute to building a reputation as a composed and effective professional.

Chapter 3: Salary Negotiation

When To Broach Salary Requirements

Discussing salary requirements is a crucial aspect of the job application process, and timing is key to ensuring a positive outcome. Here's a guide on when to strategically broach the topic of salary requirements:

Initial Job Posting Assessment:

Evaluate Job Posting: Begin by thoroughly assessing the job posting. Some employers provide clear information about the salary range, while others may leave it open for discussion. Use this initial information as a guide.

Wait for Employer's Cue:

Follow the Employer's Lead: If the employer does not explicitly request salary information in the early stages of the application, it is advisable to wait for their cue. Prematurely introducing the topic may come across as presumptive.

Post-Initial Screening:

After Initial Screening: Once you've successfully passed initial screenings or interviews and have a better understanding of the company's interest in your candidacy, it becomes more appropriate to discuss salary expectations.

When You Have Sufficient Information:

Gather Sufficient Information: Broach the subject of salary requirements when you have gathered sufficient information about the role, responsibilities, and the company's expectations. This enables you to tailor your response more effectively.

During a Formal Interview:

Formal Interview Stage: As you progress through the interview stages and the employer expresses continued interest, consider discussing salary requirements during a formal interview. This is an opportune time to align expectations.

When the Job Offer Is Imminent:

Prior to Job Offer: Ideally, initiate discussions about salary before a formal job offer is extended. This ensures that both parties are on the same page, minimizing surprises during the final stages of the hiring process.

After Highlighting Your Value:

After Demonstrating Value: Discuss salary requirements after you've had the opportunity to highlight your skills, experiences, and the value you bring to the role. This positions you as a strong candidate before diving into specifics.

When Employer Raises the Topic:

Responding to Employer Inquiry: If the employer raises the topic of salary expectations during an interview, be prepared to respond confidently. Articulate your expectations based on thorough research and industry standards.

Upon Request for Salary History:

Responding to Salary History Requests: Some employers may request your salary history. If uncomfortable providing this information, consider redirecting the conversation towards your salary expectations for the new role.

In a Collaborative Manner:

Frame as Collaboration: Broach the topic of salary requirements in a collaborative manner, expressing your eagerness to find a mutually beneficial arrangement. Emphasize your commitment to contributing value to the organization.

Consider Regional Variances:

Account for Regional Differences: If applying for positions in different regions, consider the cost of living variations. Adjust your salary expectations accordingly, accounting for regional differences in living expenses.

After Researching Industry Standards:

Backed by Research: Ensure your salary requirements are backed by thorough research on industry standards, considering your experience, skills, and the specific demands of the role.

When Negotiations Are Imminent:

Entering Negotiation Phase: If you sense that negotiations are imminent, feel free to initiate a conversation about salary requirements. This proactive approach demonstrates your readiness for the next stages of the hiring process.

After Building Rapport:

Established Relationship: Once you've established a rapport with the employer and have a clearer understanding of the company culture, feel confident in discussing salary requirements as part of the broader conversation about your fit within the organization.

Prior to Finalizing Terms:

Before Finalizing Terms: The final stages of the hiring process, just before the terms are formalized, are an appropriate time to ensure that both parties are aligned on salary expectations, avoiding potential misunderstandings.

Strategic timing is essential when broaching the topic of salary requirements. By carefully assessing the situation, waiting for the right cues, and choosing appropriate moments during the application process, you position yourself for a more successful negotiation and a positive start to your potential employment.

Making The Initial Salary Request

Initiating the conversation about salary expectations requires finesse and strategic communication. Here's a guide on making the initial salary request with confidence and effectiveness:

Wait for the Right Moment:

Choose Appropriate Timing: Pick a strategic moment to introduce the topic. Ideally, wait until the employer has signaled interest in moving forward with your application or during a dedicated salary discussion phase.

Express Enthusiasm First:

Convey Enthusiasm: Begin by expressing your enthusiasm for the role and the company. This sets a positive tone for the conversation and emphasizes your genuine interest in the position.

Acknowledge the Company's Investment:

Acknowledge Investment: Recognize the employer's investment in the hiring process and convey your excitement about the prospect of contributing to the organization's success.

Highlight Your Value:

Reinforce Your Value Proposition: Remind the employer of the unique value you bring to the role. Emphasize specific skills, experiences, and achievements that make you a strong candidate.

Conduct Thorough Research:

Research Industry Standards: Prior to making your request, conduct thorough research on industry salary standards for your role, considering factors such as experience, location, and company size.

Determine Your Desired Range:

Establish a Range: Determine a realistic salary range based on your research, experience, and the specific demands of the role. Be prepared to justify the figures within this range.

Consider Total Compensation:

Factor in Benefits and Perks: When making your initial request, consider not only the base salary but also the overall compensation package, including benefits, bonuses, and any other perks.

Use a Range Instead of a Specific Number:

Offer a Range: Presenting a salary range instead of a specific number allows for flexibility. It also provides room for negotiation while still communicating your expectations.

Be Transparent but Tactful:

Transparent Communication: Be transparent about your salary expectations, but do so tactfully. Phrase your request in a way that conveys flexibility and a willingness to engage in a collaborative discussion.

Consider the Company's Budget:

Alignment with Company Budget: While advocating for your own needs, be mindful of the company's budget constraints. Demonstrating awareness and flexibility can positively influence the negotiation process.

Use Professional Language:

Formal and Professional Tone: Frame your request in a formal and professional manner. Avoid informal language and focus on creating a business-like atmosphere during the negotiation.

Discuss Room for Growth:

Reference Career Advancement: If appropriate, express your interest in discussing opportunities for career advancement and professional development. This reinforces your commitment to long-term collaboration.

Be Ready for a Counteroffer:

Anticipate Negotiation: Understand that your initial request may be met with a counteroffer. Be prepared to engage in a constructive negotiation, emphasizing collaboration and mutual benefit.

Express Willingness to Discuss:

Openness to Discussion: Clearly communicate your openness to further discuss and negotiate the salary package. This fosters a collaborative atmosphere and demonstrates your commitment to finding a mutually beneficial agreement.

Follow Up with Justification if Required:

Provide Justification if Asked: If the employer seeks justification for your salary request, be ready to provide evidence of your qualifications, relevant experience, and industry benchmarks that support your expectations.

Remember, making the initial salary request is a significant step in the negotiation process. By approaching it strategically, you set the stage for a constructive discussion that aligns your expcctations with the employer's while showcasing your value to the organization.

Negotiating A Raise Or Promotion Pay

Negotiating a raise or promotion can be a pivotal moment in your career, requiring a strategic approach and effective communication. Here's a comprehensive guide to help you navigate this important process:

Prepare Thoroughly:

Gather Information: Before initiating the negotiation, gather relevant information. Research industry salary standards, evaluate your contributions to the company, and understand the expectations for your current or new role.

Highlight Achievements:

Emphasize Contributions: Articulate your key achievements and contributions to the organization. Quantify your impact wherever possible, demonstrating the value you bring to the team and the company as a whole.

Timing is Crucial:

Choose the Right Time: Timing is essential when negotiating a raise or promotion. Ideally, initiate discussions after accomplishing significant milestones or when the company is in a positive financial state.

Express Your Interest:

Convey Career Ambitions: Clearly express your interest in advancing within the company. Discuss your commitment to long-term growth and how the proposed raise or promotion aligns with your career goals.

Understand Company Policies:

Familiarize Yourself: Be aware of the company's policies regarding salary adjustments and promotions. Understanding the standard procedures helps you navigate the negotiation process more effectively.

Quantify Your Value:

Use Data and Metrics: Support your negotiation with data and metrics. Demonstrate how your performance has positively impacted the company's success, emphasizing any measurable outcomes or improvements.

Craft a Compelling Proposal:

Present a Proposal: Prepare a well-crafted proposal that outlines your achievements, the responsibilities you've shouldered, and the reasons you deserve the raise or promotion. This document serves as a structured guide during discussions.

Know Your Market Value:

Research Market Salaries: Understand your market value in terms of salary. Research salaries for similar roles in your industry and location to ensure your expectations are in line with current standards.

Practice Effective Communication:

Clear and Confident Communication: Practice clear and confident communication. Articulate your points with clarity, emphasizing your passion for your role and your dedication to contributing to the company's success.

Demonstrate Continued Learning:

Highlight Professional Development: Showcase any additional skills or certifications you've acquired since your last review. Illustrate your commitment to continuous learning and how it benefits the company.

Consider Non-Monetary Benefits:

Evaluate Non-Monetary Perks: If a salary increase is challenging, consider negotiating for non-monetary benefits such as flexible work hours, additional vacation days, or professional development opportunities.

Stay Positive and Professional:

Maintain a Positive Tone: Throughout the negotiation, maintain a positive and professional demeanor. Focus on the future and your commitment to contributing to the company's success.

Be Open to Compromise:

Flexibility in Negotiation: Be open to compromise. If the initial proposal isn't fully accepted, explore alternative solutions that may satisfy both parties. A willingness to find common ground demonstrates maturity.

Ask for Feedback:

Seek Constructive Feedback: If the employer is hesitant, ask for constructive feedback on areas where improvement is needed. Use this information to formulate a plan for addressing any concerns.

Follow Up in Writing:

Formalize the Agreement: If a verbal agreement is reached, promptly follow up in writing. Send a formal email summarizing the key points discussed, including the agreed-upon salary or promotion terms, to avoid misunderstandings.

Continue to Excel:

Maintain High Performance: After securing the raise or promotion, continue to excel in your role. Demonstrate that the investment made by the company in your career growth was well-placed.

Negotiating a raise or promotion is a critical skill that can significantly impact your professional trajectory. By approaching the process with preparation, effective communication, and a collaborative mindset, you increase the likelihood of a successful outcome that aligns with your career goals.

Following Up After The Offer

Securing a job offer is a significant achievement, but your journey doesn't end there. Properly following up is essential to ensure a smooth transition into your new role and maintain a positive impression. Here's a comprehensive guide on how to follow up after receiving a job offer:

Express Gratitude Immediately:

Prompt Thank-You Email: Send a thank-you email promptly after receiving the offer. Express your gratitude for the opportunity, convey your excitement about joining the team, and reiterate your appreciation for being selected.

Request Clarifications if Needed:

Seek Additional Information: If any details about the offer are unclear, don't hesitate to seek clarification. Request additional information on aspects such as start date, benefits, or any other terms that require clarification.

Confirm Acceptance and Terms:

Formal Acceptance: Once you're ready to accept the offer, confirm your acceptance formally. Restate the agreed-upon terms, such as salary, benefits, and start date, to ensure both parties are on the same page.

Coordinate Logistics:

Initiate Onboarding Process: Inquire about the onboarding process and necessary documentation. Coordinate logistics such as paperwork, orientation schedules, and any pre-employment requirements.

Express Enthusiasm for Onboarding:

Eager Anticipation: Convey your enthusiasm for the onboarding process. Express your eagerness to integrate into the team, learn about the company culture, and contribute to the organization's success.

Check-in on Next Steps:

Inquire About Next Steps: Ask about the next steps in the hiring process. Seek information on any additional paperwork, orientations, or meetings that may be scheduled before your official start date.

Confirm Start Date and Time:

Verify Start Details: Double-check the start date, time, and location of your first day. Ensure that you have a clear understanding of where to report and any preparations you need to make for a smooth onboarding experience.

Express Willingness to Prepare:

Preparation Readiness: Assure the employer of your readiness for onboarding. Express your willingness to prepare in advance by completing any pre-employment tasks or training modules provided.

Notify Other Prospective Employers:

Inform Other Prospective Employers: If you were considering multiple job offers, promptly inform the other prospective employers of your decision. Maintain professionalism and gratitude in your communications.

Initiate Communication with HR:

Contact Human Resources: Reach out to the Human Resources department or the designated contact person. Introduce yourself, express your excitement about joining the company, and inquire about any additional information or paperwork required.

Connect with Future Colleagues:

Reach Out to Team Members: If possible, connect with your future colleagues. Express your excitement to be part of the team and inquire if there are any preliminary introductions or materials you should review before starting.

Prepare Any Necessary Documentation:

Gather Required Documents: Prepare any necessary documentation requested by the company, such as identification, work authorization, or certifications. Ensure that you have everything ready for a smooth onboarding process.

Express Appreciation to Hiring Manager:

Thank the Hiring Manager: Extend your appreciation to the hiring manager or key decision-makers. Reiterate your enthusiasm for the role and your gratitude for the opportunity to contribute to the organization.

Clarify Remote Work Arrangements:

Discuss Remote Work Details: If your role involves remote work, clarify expectations regarding equipment, communication tools, and any policies related to remote work. Ensure you are well-prepared for a seamless virtual onboarding experience.

Stay Proactive and Responsive:

Proactive Communication: Stay proactive and responsive to any communication from the company. Promptly reply to emails, complete required paperwork, and demonstrate your commitment to a smooth onboarding process.

Prepare for a Smooth Transition:

Transition Planning: If you are transitioning from another job, ensure a smooth handover of responsibilities. Communicate with your current employer and colleagues, providing ample notice and facilitating a seamless transition.

Following up after a job offer is not just about accepting the position but also about laying the foundation for a positive and successful journey with your new employer. By expressing gratitude, seeking clarifications, and preparing diligently for the onboarding process, you set the stage for a smooth transition into your new role.

Types Of Benefits To Consider

When evaluating job opportunities, considering the full spectrum of benefits is crucial. Beyond the base salary, employers often provide a range of benefits that contribute to overall compensation and work-life balance. Here are key types of benefits to consider when assessing a job offer:

Health Insurance:

Medical Coverage: Comprehensive health insurance plans cover medical expenses, including doctor visits, hospital stays, prescriptions, and preventive care. Evaluate the coverage, deductibles, and co-payments.

Dental and Vision Insurance:

Oral and Eye Care: Dental and vision insurance plans can help cover expenses related to dental procedures and vision care, including eye exams, glasses, and contact lenses.

Retirement Plans:

401(k) or Pension Plans: Employer-sponsored retirement plans, such as 401(k)s or pension plans, enable employees to contribute a portion of their salary toward retirement savings, often with employer matching contributions.

Life Insurance:

Financial Protection: Life insurance provides financial protection for employees and their families in the event of the employee's death. Employers may offer basic coverage or allow employees to purchase additional coverage.

Disability Insurance:

Income Protection: Disability insurance replaces a portion of an employee's income if they become unable to work due to illness or injury. Short-term and long-term disability coverage may be provided.

Flexible Spending Accounts (FSAs) and Health Savings Accounts (HSAs):

Tax-Advantaged Savings: FSAs and HSAs allow employees to set aside pre-tax dollars for eligible medical expenses. HSAs, in particular, are linked to high-deductible health plans and can be used for both current and future healthcare costs.

Paid Time Off (PTO):

Vacation and Sick Leave: PTO encompasses vacation days, holidays, and sick leave. Evaluate the company's policy on accrual, carryover, and flexibility in taking time off.

Parental Leave:

Support for New Parents: Parental leave policies vary, but many companies offer paid or unpaid leave for new parents. Consider the duration and flexibility of parental leave options.

Remote Work and Flexibility:

Work-Life Balance: The option to work remotely or have flexible work hours contributes to a healthy work-life balance. Assess the company's policies regarding remote work and flexibility.

Professional Development:

Training and Education Assistance: Companies may offer opportunities for professional development, including training programs, workshops, conferences, and financial assistance for continuing education.

Employee Assistance Programs (EAPs):

Mental Health and Counseling: EAPs provide confidential counseling and support services for employees dealing with personal or work-related challenges, contributing to overall well-being.

Wellness Programs:

Health and Fitness Initiatives: Wellness programs promote employee health through activities, resources, and incentives. This may include gym memberships, fitness classes, or wellness challenges.

Employee Discounts:

Cost-Saving Opportunities: Some employers provide discounts on company products or services, or partner with external businesses to offer exclusive discounts to employees.

Transportation Benefits:

Commuter Benefits: Companies may offer benefits to help employees with commuting costs, such as transit passes, parking reimbursements, or bike-sharing memberships.

Tuition Reimbursement:

Educational Support: *Tuition reimbursement* programs assist employees pursuing further education. Evaluate the eligibility criteria and reimbursement limits.

Recognition and Rewards Programs:

Acknowledgment for Achievements: Recognition programs acknowledge employees for their achievements and milestones. This can include awards, bonuses, or other forms of appreciation.

Legal Assistance and Insurance:

Legal Support: Some employers offer legal assistance programs or insurance plans to help employees with legal matters, such as estate planning or identity theft protection.

Relocation Assistance:

Support for Relocating Employees: Companies may provide assistance for employees relocating for a job, including reimbursement for moving expenses or temporary housing.

Comprehensive Training Programs:

Skills Development: Robust training programs support employees in developing new skills, staying updated on industry trends, and enhancing their professional capabilities.

Employee Social Events and Perks:

Team Building and Morale Boosters: Social events, team-building activities, and perks like free snacks contribute to a positive work environment and employee morale.

Considering these types of benefits holistically allows you to assess the overall value of a job offer and make informed decisions that align with your personal and professional priorities.

Healthcare, retirement, paid leave negotiation

Negotiating healthcare, retirement, and paid leave benefits is a crucial aspect of securing a comprehensive compensation package. Here's a strategic guide to help you navigate negotiations in these key areas:

Healthcare Negotiation:

Understand the Health Insurance Offering:

Comprehensive Review: Thoroughly review the offered health insurance plan. Assess coverage, deductibles, co-payments, and the network of healthcare providers. Identify any potential gaps in coverage.

Consider Family Needs:

Evaluate Family Coverage: If applicable, consider the needs of your family. Assess the cost and coverage of adding dependents to the health insurance plan. Ensure that the plan aligns with your family's healthcare requirements.

Negotiate Premiums and Contributions:

Premium Adjustment: Inquire about the possibility of premium adjustments. While some companies have fixed contribution amounts, others may be open to negotiation, especially if you can demonstrate competitive offerings from other employers.

Explore Additional Health Benefits:

Wellness Programs: Inquire about additional health benefits such as wellness programs, gym memberships, or preventive care initiatives. Some employers offer incentives for participating in wellness activities.

Flexible Spending Accounts (FSAs) and Health Savings Accounts (HSAs):

Negotiate Contribution Limits: If the company offers FSAs or HSAs, discuss contribution limits. Negotiate for higher limits to maximize tax advantages for medical expenses.

Retirement Plan Negotiation:

Understand the Retirement Plan:

Detailed Review: Examine the details of the retirement plan, whether it's a 401(k), pension, or another type. Assess employer matching contributions, vesting schedules, and investment options.

Negotiate Matching Contributions:

Matching Adjustment: If the employer offers a matching contribution, discuss the possibility of increasing the match percentage or adjusting the vesting schedule. This can significantly impact your long-term retirement savings.

Explore Additional Retirement Benefits:

Supplemental Plans: Inquire about any supplemental retirement benefits, such as profit-sharing or employee stock purchase plans. Negotiate for additional perks that contribute to your financial well-being.

Discuss Rollover Options:

Portability: If you have retirement funds from a previous employer, discuss options for rolling them into the new plan. Some employers may offer assistance in this process.

Paid Leave Negotiation:

Understand Existing Paid Leave Policies:

Policy Review: Familiarize yourself with the company's existing paid leave policies, including vacation, sick leave, and public holidays. Understand the accrual rates and any restrictions on usage.

Negotiate Vacation Days:

Additional Vacation Days: Negotiate for additional vacation days if the standard offering is below industry averages or if you have specific personal or family needs that require extra time off.

Explore Flexibility in Leave Usage:

Flexible Leave Policies: Inquire about flexibility in leave usage. Some companies may allow employees to take half-days or flexible hours to accommodate personal needs without exhausting full-day leave.

Discuss Paid Family Leave:

Family-Oriented Benefits: If family considerations are important to you, discuss the possibility of additional paid family leave, especially for parental or caregiving responsibilities.

Clarify Sick Leave Policies:

Robust Sick Leave: Ensure that the sick leave policy aligns with your expectations. Discuss the potential for additional sick days or flexibility in using sick leave for personal wellness days.

Negotiate Public Holiday Policies:

Holiday Flexibility: If the company has rigid policies regarding public holidays, negotiate for flexibility. Some employees may prefer to work on certain holidays and take alternate days off.

General Tips for Successful Benefit Negotiations:

Market Research:

Benchmark Against Industry Standards: Conduct thorough research on industry benchmarks for healthcare, retirement, and paid leave benefits. Use this information to justify your negotiation requests.

Emphasize Your Value:

Highlight Your Contributions: Emphasize your contributions to the company and how your skills and experience make you an asset. Connect your request for enhanced benefits to your commitment and dedication.

Prioritize Flexibility:

Balancing Work and Life: Communicate the importance of work-life balance and how flexible healthcare, retirement, and leave policies contribute to your overall well-being and job satisfaction.

Timing is Key:

Strategic Timing: Choose an appropriate time for benefit negotiations. Ideally, these discussions are initiated during the final stages of the interview process or when a job offer is extended.

Be Prepared to Compromise:

Flexibility in Negotiation: Understand that negotiations involve give-and-take. Be open to compromise and explore creative solutions that address both your needs and the employer's budget constraints.

By approaching healthcare, retirement, and paid leave negotiations strategically, you enhance your overall compensation package and create a work environment that aligns with your personal and financial goals.

Educational Assistance And Tuition Reimbursement

Educational assistance and tuition reimbursement programs are valuable benefits that support employees in pursuing further education and skill development. Understanding and strategically leveraging these benefits can significantly contribute to your professional growth. Here's a comprehensive guide to navigating educational assistance and tuition reimbursement:

Educational Assistance Programs:

Definition and Purpose:

Investment in Learning: Educational assistance programs are initiatives by employers to invest in the continuous learning and development of their employees. These programs often cover a range of educational activities, from degree programs to professional certifications.

Eligibility Criteria:

Varied Eligibility: Employers may have different eligibility criteria for educational assistance programs. While some programs are available to all employees, others may have specific requirements related to job roles, tenure, or performance.

Covered Expenses:

Diverse Educational Activities: Educational assistance can cover various expenses, including tuition, fees, textbooks, and other related costs. Some programs may extend to cover the expenses of workshops, conferences, and online courses.

Application Process:

Structured Application: Employers typically have a structured application process for educational assistance. This may involve submitting a formal request, outlining the proposed educational activity, and providing details on how it aligns with professional development goals.

Approval and Documentation:

Confirmation and Documentation: Once approved, employees often receive confirmation and guidelines on documentation requirements. This may include proof of enrollment, receipts, and academic progress reports.

Tax Implications:

Tax Benefits: Some educational assistance programs offer tax benefits for both the employer and the employee. Be aware of the tax implications, and consider consulting with a tax professional to maximize available benefits.

Tuition Reimbursement:

Purpose and Scope:

Financial Support for Tuition: Tuition reimbursement specifically focuses on covering the costs associated with pursuing a degree or certification. Employers may reimburse a portion or the full amount of tuition expenses.

Reimbursement Limits:

Defined Reimbursement Limits: Employers often set limits on the amount they are willing to reimburse annually or per course. Understand these limits and ensure your educational plans align with the available reimbursement.

Eligibility and Waiting Periods:

Clear Eligibility Requirements: Tuition reimbursement programs may have eligibility requirements, such as a minimum period of employment or successful completion of a probationary period. Be aware of any waiting periods before applying.

Approved Institutions and Programs:

Defined Institutions and Programs: Employers may have a list of approved institutions or specific programs eligible for reimbursement. Ensure that your chosen educational institution and program align with the employer's guidelines.

Maintaining Academic Standards:

Academic Performance Requirements: Tuition reimbursement programs often have academic performance requirements. Maintain the necessary standards to continue eligibility and receive reimbursements.

Reimbursement Process:

Structured Reimbursement Process: Understand the reimbursement process, including submission deadlines, required documentation, and any additional steps. Familiarize yourself with the channels through which reimbursements are processed.

Flexibility in Course Selection:

Diverse Course Options: Some tuition reimbursement programs offer flexibility in the types of courses covered. This can include undergraduate or graduate degrees, certificates, or professional development courses.

General Tips for Maximizing Educational Benefits:

Align with Career Goals:

Strategic Alignment: Choose educational activities that align with your career goals and the needs of your current or desired role within the company. Demonstrating a clear connection enhances the likelihood of approval.

Communicate Intentions Clearly:

Transparent Communication: Clearly communicate your intentions to pursue further education to your supervisor or HR department. Discuss how the educational activities will benefit both you and the organization.

Explore Internal Opportunities:

In-House Learning Opportunities: Check if the company offers internal training programs or partnerships with educational institutions. These may provide cost-effective alternatives and specific courses tailored to company needs.

Plan Ahead:

Strategic Planning: Plan your educational pursuits strategically. Consider factors such as workload, project commitments, and personal obligations to ensure a balanced approach to both work and studies.

Network and Share Insights:

Knowledge Sharing: Encourage a culture of knowledge sharing within the workplace. If you acquire new skills or insights through educational activities, share them with colleagues, contributing to a culture of continuous learning.

Evaluate Return on Investment:

Long-Term Benefits: Assess the return on investment for both you and the company. How will the newly acquired skills contribute to your role and the organization's success? Clearly articulate these benefits when seeking approval.

Stay Informed about Policies:

Policy Awareness: Stay informed about any updates or changes to the educational assistance and tuition reimbursement policies. Periodically review the terms and conditions to ensure compliance.

Build a Portfolio of Skills:

Diversify Skill Set: Use educational assistance and tuition reimbursement to diversify your skill set. Acquiring a range of skills enhances your professional versatility and adaptability.

By navigating educational assistance and tuition reimbursement strategically, you can leverage these benefits to advance your career, contribute more effectively to your organization, and foster a culture of continuous learning within your workplace.

Unique Perks And Flexible Work Arrangements

In today's dynamic work landscape, employers recognize the importance of fostering a positive and flexible work environment. Beyond traditional benefits, unique perks and flexible work arrangements play a pivotal role in enhancing employee satisfaction, well-being, and productivity. Here's a comprehensive exploration of these elements that contribute to a holistic workplace experience:

Wellness Initiatives:

Health and Fitness: Some companies offer on-site fitness facilities, wellness programs, or access to health and fitness apps. These initiatives promote physical well-being and encourage a healthy work-life balance.

Flexible Work Hours:

Adaptable Schedules: Providing flexibility in work hours allows employees to customize their schedules, accommodating personal preferences or external commitments. This promotes a sense of autonomy and work-life integration.

Casual Dress Code:

Relaxed Attire Norms: Implementing a casual dress code fosters a more relaxed and comfortable atmosphere. It can contribute to a positive workplace culture and ease the pressure of adhering to formal dress standards.

Pet-Friendly Policies:

Furry Companionship: Pet-friendly workplaces allow employees to bring their pets to the office. This unique perk can reduce stress, enhance job satisfaction, and create a more relaxed and enjoyable work environment.

Employee Recognition Programs:

Acknowledgment and Rewards: Recognition programs that celebrate employee achievements contribute to a positive workplace culture. This can include awards, shout-outs, or even small tokens of appreciation for exceptional performance.

Professional Development Opportunities:

Continuous Learning: Offering opportunities for professional development, such as workshops, conferences, or access to online courses, shows a commitment to employee growth. This can enhance skill sets and job satisfaction.

Remote Work Options:

Telecommuting Opportunities: Remote work options allow employees to work from locations outside the office. This flexibility can improve work-life balance, reduce commuting stress, and enhance overall job satisfaction.

On-Site Childcare Services:

Family-Friendly Support: On-site childcare facilities or partnerships with nearby daycare centers ease the challenges faced by working parents. This benefit demonstrates a commitment to family-friendly policies.

Financial Wellness Programs:

Guidance and Support: Providing financial wellness programs, including seminars, counseling, or assistance with budgeting, helps employees manage financial stress and promotes overall well-being.

Generous Time-Off Policies:

Extended Vacation Options: Offering generous time-off policies, such as sabbaticals or extended vacation allowances, allows employees to recharge and pursue personal interests without the fear of burnout.

Transportation Benefits:

Commute Support: Transportation perks, such as subsidized public transportation, bike-sharing memberships, or parking allowances, demonstrate an employer's commitment to easing the commuting burden.

Diversity and Inclusion Initiatives:

Inclusive Workplaces: Establishing diversity and inclusion programs fosters a sense of belonging. This can include affinity groups, mentorship programs, and initiatives that promote a diverse and inclusive workplace culture.

Social Events and Team Building:

Community Building: Organizing social events, team-building activities, and regular gatherings create a sense of community among employees. These activities contribute to a positive work culture and strengthen team relationships.

Volunteer and Giving Programs:

Social Responsibility: Encouraging volunteerism and community service through organized programs aligns the company with social responsibility. This can boost employee morale and engagement.

Flexible Work Arrangements:

Remote Work:

Anywhere Productivity: Remote work allows employees to perform their duties from locations outside the traditional office, promoting flexibility and accommodating diverse work styles.

Flextime:

Adaptable Work Hours: Flextime enables employees to choose when they start and end their workday, providing autonomy in managing their schedules while ensuring they meet job requirements.

Compressed Workweeks:

Condensed Work Schedule: Compressed workweeks involve completing the standard work hours within fewer days, offering extended weekends or additional days off.

Job Sharing:

Shared Responsibilities: Job sharing involves two or more employees sharing the responsibilities of a single full-time position, allowing for a flexible division of tasks and work hours.

Part-Time Work:

Reduced Hours: Part-time arrangements involve working fewer hours than a standard full-time schedule, accommodating individuals who seek a better work-life balance or have other commitments.

Flexible Location Policies:

Geographic Independence: Providing flexibility in choosing work locations allows employees to work from various places, including co-working spaces, cafes, or even different offices.

Phased Retirement:

Gradual Transition: Phased retirement enables older employees to gradually reduce their work hours or responsibilities as they approach retirement, facilitating a smoother transition.

Annualized Hours:

Flexible Annual Schedules: Annualized hours allow employees to work a certain number of hours over the course of a year, providing flexibility in distributing workloads based on seasonal demands.

Shift Swapping:

Collaborative Scheduling: Shift swapping enables employees to exchange work shifts with colleagues, accommodating personal needs or unexpected circumstances without affecting productivity.

Flexibility Agreements:

Customized Arrangements: Establishing flexibility agreements that tailor work arrangements to individual needs, such as phased returns from maternity leave or temporary adjustments, demonstrates a commitment to employee well-being.

General Tips for Maximizing Unique Perks and Flexible Work Arrangements:

Align with Personal Values:

Choose Perks that Matter: Select unique perks and flexible arrangements that align with your personal values and priorities, contributing to a work environment that enhances your overall well-being.

Effective Communication:

Clear Communication: Communicate openly with supervisors and HR regarding your preferences for unique perks or flexible work arrangements. Effective communication ensures a mutual understanding of expectations.

Explore Organizational Culture:

Assess Workplace Culture: Consider how unique perks and flexible work arrangements align with the organizational culture. Companies that prioritize these aspects tend to foster a positive and supportive work environment.

Balance Work and Personal Needs:

Strategic Balance: Strive for a balance that meets both your professional and personal needs. Select perks or arrangements that contribute positively to your work-life integration.

Evaluate Long-Term Impact:

Consider Future Implications: Assess the long-term impact of unique perks and flexible arrangements on your career trajectory. Choose options that align with your goals and contribute positively to your professional growth.

Stay Informed about Policies:

Policy Awareness: Stay informed about any updates or changes to unique perks and flexible work arrangement policies. Regularly review and understand the terms and conditions to ensure compliance.

Encourage Inclusivity:

Promote Inclusive Practices: Advocate for inclusive practices within the workplace. Encourage the adoption of unique perks and flexible arrangements that cater to diverse needs and contribute to a more inclusive culture.

Share Feedback:

Provide Constructive Feedback: If certain perks or arrangements can be improved or adjusted, share constructive feedback with the relevant departments. Continuous improvement enhances the overall workplace experience.

By embracing unique perks and flexible work arrangements, employees and organizations can create a dynamic and supportive workplace that nurtures individual well-being, boosts morale, and fosters a culture of adaptability and innovation.

Evaluating The Overall Compensation Package

Assessing the overall compensation package is a critical step in making informed decisions about your employment. Beyond the base salary, a comprehensive evaluation involves considering benefits, bonuses, and other perks. Here's a detailed guide to help you navigate the process of evaluating your overall compensation package:

Base Salary:

Benchmarking: Begin by assessing the base salary offered. Research industry standards, considering factors such as your experience, skills, and the cost of living in the location where you'll be working.

Bonuses and Incentives:

Variable Compensation: Examine the structure of bonuses and incentives. Understand whether they are performance-based, annual, or tied to specific achievements. Evaluate the potential impact on your overall income.

Healthcare Benefits:

Medical Coverage: Review the healthcare benefits, including health insurance coverage, deductibles, and co-payments. Assess the comprehensiveness of the plan and its alignment with your medical needs.

Retirement Plans:

Contributions and Matching: Evaluate the employer's contributions to retirement plans, such as 401(k) or pension plans. Consider the matching percentage and vesting schedule, as these factors impact your long-term financial health.

Stock Options and Equity:

Equity Participation: If offered, examine stock options or equity grants. Understand the vesting schedule, potential for growth, and how these elements contribute to your overall financial portfolio.

Paid Time Off (PTO):

Vacation and Sick Leave: Assess the PTO policy, including the allocation of vacation days, sick leave, and any additional leave options. Consider how well it aligns with your work-life balance preferences.

Flexible Work Arrangements:

Work-Life Integration: Evaluate any flexible work arrangements offered, such as remote work options, flextime, or compressed workweeks. Consider how these align with your preferred work style.

Educational Assistance and Tuition Reimbursement:

Investment in Learning: Examine any educational assistance or tuition reimbursement programs. Assess how these programs support your professional development and contribute to your long-term goals.

Performance Reviews and Career Advancement:

Growth Opportunities: Inquire about the performance review process and opportunities for career advancement. Understand how performance evaluations impact salary increases, promotions, and professional development.

Employee Recognition and Rewards:

Acknowledgment Programs: Evaluate any employee recognition and rewards programs. Recognition for achievements contributes to job satisfaction and can be a valuable component of the overall compensation experience.

Wellness Programs:

Health and Well-being Initiatives: Consider any wellness programs offered, such as gym memberships, mental health support, or wellness challenges. These initiatives contribute to a healthy and supportive work environment.

Childcare and Family Benefits:

Family-Friendly Policies: If applicable, assess childcare and family benefits. These may include on-site childcare services, parental leave policies, or other family-oriented perks.

Career Development Opportunities:

Training and Advancement: Review opportunities for career development, including training programs, mentorship initiatives, and promotions. Consider how the company invests in your professional growth.

Diversity and Inclusion Initiatives:

Inclusive Workplace Culture: Evaluate diversity and inclusion initiatives. A workplace that values diversity fosters a more inclusive and supportive culture.

Cost of Living Adjustments:

Geographic Considerations: If applicable, assess whether the compensation package includes adjustments for the cost of living in the location where you'll be working. This ensures that your income is competitive in the local market.

Employee Assistance Programs (EAPs):

Support Services: Check for the availability of employee assistance programs that provide confidential counseling and support services. These can contribute to overall well-being.

Legal Assistance and Insurance:

Legal Support: If offered, evaluate legal assistance programs or insurance plans. These can be valuable for addressing legal matters or protecting against identity theft.

Transportation and Commute Benefits:

Commute Support: Assess transportation benefits, such as subsidized public transportation, parking allowances, or bike-sharing memberships. These perks ease the commuting burden.

Employee Discounts:

Cost-Saving Opportunities: Review any employee discount programs for company products or services. These perks can contribute to your overall financial well-being.

Communication and Transparency:

Clarity and Openness: Evaluate the company's communication and transparency regarding the compensation package. A clear understanding of the terms and conditions fosters trust and satisfaction.

General Tips for Evaluation:

Prioritize Your Needs:

Identify Priorities: Prioritize elements of the compensation package based on your personal and professional needs. Focus on what matters most to you and aligns with your goals.

Consider the Full Picture:

Holistic Perspective: Evaluate the compensation package as a whole rather than focusing solely on salary. Consider how each component contributes to your overall job satisfaction and well-being.

Ask Questions:

Clarify Doubts: Don't hesitate to ask questions about any aspect of the compensation package that is unclear. Seek clarification on policies, benefits, and expectations to make an informed decision.

Negotiate Strategically:

Effective Negotiation: If certain aspects of the compensation package can be improved, approach negotiations strategically. Present your case, backed by research and a clear understanding of your value to the organization.

Future Considerations:

Long-Term Implications: Consider the long-term implications of the compensation package. How does it align with your career goals, and does it offer opportunities for growth and advancement?

Market Benchmarking:

Stay Informed: Continuously benchmark your compensation against industry standards. This ensures that you remain competitive in the job market and are aware of evolving trends.

Seek Professional Advice:

Consult Professionals: If needed, seek advice from HR professionals, career counselors, or financial advisors. Their insights can provide valuable perspectives on your overall compensation package.

Evaluate Company Culture:

Cultural Fit: Assess how the compensation package aligns with the company's culture. A workplace that values its employees and promotes a positive culture contributes to overall job satisfaction.

In conclusion, evaluating the overall compensation package requires a thorough examination of various components beyond the base salary. Taking a holistic approach, considering your personal and professional priorities, and seeking clarity on each element will empower you to make informed decisions about your employment.

Negotiating Non-Competes And Stock Options

Negotiating employment terms involves careful consideration of non-compete agreements and stock options, both of which significantly impact your professional trajectory. Here's a comprehensive guide to help you navigate the negotiation process for non-competes and stock options:

Negotiating Non-Compete Agreements:

Understand the Terms:

Review Cautiously: Carefully review the terms of the non-compete agreement. Pay attention to its scope, duration, geographical limitations, and specific restrictions on your post-employment activities.

Evaluate Enforceability:

Legal Consultation: If feasible, seek legal advice to evaluate the enforceability of the non-compete agreement. Different jurisdictions have varying laws regarding the validity and enforceability of such agreements.

Define Scope and Restrictions:

Narrow Down Restrictions: If the non-compete is overly broad, consider negotiating to narrow down its scope and restrictions. Focus on tailoring the agreement to protect the legitimate interests of the employer without hindering your future career opportunities.

Negotiate Compensation:

Compensation for Restrictions: If the non-compete imposes significant restrictions on your ability to work in the industry, negotiate for compensation during the restricted period. This could include a continuation of salary, benefits, or a lump-sum payment.

Limitation on Clients or Industries:

Specify Limitations: Negotiate to limit the non-compete's applicability to specific clients, industries, or types of work. This allows you more flexibility while still addressing the concerns of the employer.

Negotiate Geographic Limitations:

Geographical Constraints: If the non-compete includes broad geographical restrictions, negotiate to narrow them down to regions directly relevant to the employer's business interests.

Request a Sunset Clause:

Time-Limited Restriction: Propose a sunset clause that gradually reduces the scope of the non-compete over time. This can be an effective compromise that addresses the employer's concerns while providing you with increased freedom over the years.

Discuss Garden Leave:

Paid Leave Period: Suggest the inclusion of a garden leave clause, which requires the employer to pay your salary during the non-compete period. This can be an alternative to an outright restriction on your ability to work.

Alternative Dispute Resolution:

Mediation or Arbitration: If there are concerns about potential disputes regarding the non-compete, propose the inclusion of alternative dispute resolution mechanisms, such as mediation or arbitration, to resolve conflicts more amicably.

Negotiating Stock Options:

Understand the Terms of Options:

Comprehensive Review: Thoroughly understand the terms of the stock options offered, including the vesting schedule, exercise price, and any conditions associated with exercising the options.

Assess Vesting Schedule:

Negotiate Vesting Terms: If the vesting schedule is lengthy, negotiate for a more favorable arrangement. This could involve accelerated vesting based on performance milestones, tenure, or other mutually agreed-upon criteria.

Evaluate Exercise Price:

Fair Valuation: Assess the fairness of the exercise price. Negotiate if you believe the valuation does not accurately reflect the company's current or projected value.

Acceleration of Vesting:

Trigger Events: Discuss the possibility of accelerated vesting in the event of a change in control, acquisition, or other trigger events. This provides protection and ensures you can realize the value of your options under specific circumstances.

Performance Metrics:

Tie to Performance: If applicable, negotiate the inclusion of performance metrics tied to stock option grants. This aligns your incentives with the company's success and may lead to additional grants for exceptional performance.

Stock Option Renewal:

Renewal Opportunities: Negotiate provisions that allow for the renewal or extension of stock options. This can be especially beneficial if the original options are set to expire before you can fully realize their value.

Transferability of Options:

Transfer or Assignment: If the stock options are non-transferable, discuss the possibility of allowing transfer or assignment, particularly in the context of mergers, acquisitions, or estate planning.

Negotiate Terms for Departure:

Treatment upon Departure: Clarify the terms regarding stock options in the event of departure, whether voluntary or involuntary. Negotiate for favorable treatment, such as extended exercise periods or accelerated vesting under certain circumstances.

Rights to Dividends and Voting:

Additional Rights: Discuss any rights to dividends or voting associated with the stock options. Negotiate to ensure you receive these additional benefits, enhancing the overall value of your stock options.

Tax Implications:

Understand Tax Consequences: Be aware of the tax implications of stock options. If possible, negotiate for structures that minimize tax burdens or provide tax advantages.

Communication and Transparency:

Open Dialogue: Maintain open communication with the employer regarding stock options. Seek transparency on the company's performance, future plans, and any changes that may impact the value of your options.

Seek Legal Advice:

Legal Consultation: Before finalizing any stock option agreement, seek legal advice to ensure a clear understanding of the terms and potential implications. Legal professionals can guide you on protecting your interests.

General Tips for Successful Negotiation:

Thorough Research:

Industry Standards: Research industry standards for non-competes and stock options to ensure your negotiation positions are informed and reasonable.

Prioritize Key Points:

Identify Priorities: Determine the most critical aspects of non-competes and stock options that align with your career goals. Prioritize these during negotiations.

Effective Communication:

Clear Expression: Clearly articulate your concerns, preferences, and any counterproposals during negotiations. Effective communication fosters a collaborative approach.

Mutual Benefit Approach:

Win-Win Solutions: Approach negotiations with a mindset of creating win-win solutions. Seek outcomes that address both your needs and the employer's concerns.

Legal Guidance:

Consult Legal Professionals: Engage legal professionals who specialize in employment law to provide guidance and ensure your interests are protected.

Flexibility and Compromise:

Be Open to Compromise: Recognize that negotiations often involve compromise. Be flexible and open to finding middle ground that satisfies both parties.

Build Positive Relationships:

Foster Collaboration: Cultivate positive relationships during negotiations. A collaborative approach builds goodwill and sets a positive tone for your professional relationship.

Review the Entire Offer:

Holistic Assessment: Consider non-competes and stock options within the context of the entire job offer. A holistic assessment ensures a comprehensive understanding of your overall compensation and benefits.

Navigating non-competes and stock options requires a strategic and informed approach. By thoroughly understanding the terms, seeking legal advice, and engaging in open and transparent communication, you can negotiate agreements that align with your career goals and contribute to a mutually beneficial professional relationship.

Securing Agreements In Writing

In any professional negotiation or agreement, securing terms in writing is a crucial step to provide clarity, mitigate misunderstandings, and establish a legally binding record. Whether dealing with employment contracts, business agreements, or any other arrangement, documenting the terms in writing ensures a solid foundation for a successful and transparent relationship. Here's a comprehensive guide on the importance of securing agreements in writing:

Clarity and Precision:

Avoid Ambiguity: A written agreement eliminates ambiguity and ensures that all parties have a clear understanding of the terms. Precise language helps prevent misinterpretation and sets a framework for expectations.

Legal Validity:

Enforceability: A written agreement holds legal weight and is generally more enforceable than verbal agreements. In the event of a dispute, a written record serves as evidence of the agreed-upon terms.

Detailed Terms and Conditions:

Comprehensive Coverage: A written agreement allows for the inclusion of detailed terms and conditions. This may include specific responsibilities, timelines, payment terms, deliverables, and any other pertinent details relevant to the agreement.

Protection for All Parties:

Mutual Safeguards: A well-drafted agreement protects the interests of all parties involved. It outlines each party's rights, obligations, and liabilities, reducing the risk of misunderstandings or disputes.

Reference Point for Disputes:

Dispute Resolution: In the event of a disagreement, a written agreement serves as a reference point for dispute resolution. It helps parties revisit the original terms and facilitates a more efficient resolution process.

Building Trust:

Demonstrate Commitment: Providing a written agreement demonstrates a commitment to the agreed-upon terms. It builds trust between parties by showcasing a shared understanding and commitment to fulfilling respective obligations.

Legal Compliance:

Ensure Legal Compliance: Written agreements help ensure that the terms comply with legal requirements and regulations. This is especially crucial in areas such as employment contracts, where legal compliance is paramount.

Future Reference:

Record for Future Use: Written agreements serve as a valuable record for future reference. They provide a historical account of the terms agreed upon, which can be useful for future collaborations, expansions, or modifications.

Prevents Memory Bias:

Avoid Memory Distortions: Memories can fade or be subject to bias over time. Having a written agreement prevents memory distortions and ensures that both parties have an accurate record of the agreed-upon terms.

Professionalism:

Professional Image: Documenting agreements in writing enhances professionalism. It reflects a serious and organized approach to business, fostering a positive impression on clients, partners, or employees.

Flexibility and Adaptability:

Allow for Modifications: While providing a clear structure, written agreements can also include clauses that allow for modifications or amendments under certain conditions. This flexibility is valuable as circumstances may change over time.

Establishing Deadlines:

Define Timelines: In contracts and agreements, written documentation establishes specific deadlines for deliverables, payments, or other milestones. This ensures that all parties are aligned on the timing of various obligations.

Consistency with Verbal Agreements:

Align with Verbal Understandings: If there have been prior verbal agreements or discussions, documenting the terms in writing helps ensure that the written agreement aligns with those verbal understandings, leaving no room for discrepancies.

Independent Legal Advice:

Encourage Independent Legal Review: Encourage all parties involved to seek independent legal advice before signing a written agreement. This ensures that each party fully understands the implications and consequences of the terms.

Confidentiality and Non-Disclosure:

Secure Confidential Information: For agreements involving sensitive information, a written agreement often includes confidentiality or non-disclosure clauses, providing an additional layer of protection for proprietary or confidential data.

Electronic Signatures and Digital Records:

Utilize Technology: In the digital age, electronic signatures and digital records have become widely accepted. Utilize secure platforms to facilitate the electronic signing and storage of agreements.

Communication of Expectations:

Set Clear Expectations: Documenting agreements in writing communicates clear expectations to all parties involved. It serves as a reference point for performance standards and ensures that everyone is on the same page.

Insurance and Liability Coverage:

Address Insurance and Liability: For contracts involving services, written agreements often specify insurance coverage and liability limits, providing a clear understanding of the financial responsibility in case of unforeseen events.

Acknowledgment of Terms:

Confirmation of Acceptance: A written agreement typically includes a section for all parties to acknowledge their understanding and acceptance of the terms. This acknowledgment is integral to the contract's validity.

Record Retention:

Maintain Records: Properly store and maintain records of all written agreements. This ensures accessibility for future reference, audits, or legal requirements.

Conclusion:

Securing agreements in writing is a fundamental practice for establishing clear expectations, reducing risks, and fostering trust in professional relationships. Whether dealing with contracts, partnerships, or employment terms, the act of documenting agreements serves as a cornerstone for transparent and legally binding collaborations.

Celebrating Successful Negotiations

Celebrating successful negotiations is a vital step in recognizing the collective efforts, achieving shared goals, and solidifying positive relationships. It not only marks the conclusion of a mutually beneficial agreement but also sets the stage for continued collaboration and strengthened partnerships. Here's a guide on how to celebrate and acknowledge the success of negotiations:

Expressing Gratitude:

Sincere Appreciation: Begin by expressing gratitude to all parties involved. Acknowledge the time, effort, and commitment invested by everyone throughout the negotiation process. A sincere thank-you goes a long way in building positive rapport.

Reflecting on Achievements:

Highlight Milestones: Take time to reflect on the achievements and milestones reached during the negotiation. Whether it's reaching a consensus on terms, overcoming challenges, or achieving specific objectives, celebrating these accomplishments boosts morale.

Commemorative Announcement:

Public Recognition: Consider making a commemorative announcement to share the successful negotiation outcome with a broader audience. This could be through internal communications, press releases, or social media platforms, showcasing the positive impact of the collaboration.

Recognition Ceremony:

Formal Acknowledgment: Organize a recognition ceremony or gathering to formally acknowledge the key contributors to the negotiation process. This could include team members, stakeholders, and any external partners who played a crucial role.

Personalized Tokens of Appreciation:

Customized Gifts: Consider providing personalized tokens of appreciation, such as engraved plaques, certificates, or commemorative items. These serve as lasting reminders of the successful negotiation and the collaborative efforts involved.

Shared Success Stories:

Narrative of Success: Share success stories resulting from the negotiation. This could be in the form of case studies, testimonials, or anecdotes that highlight the positive outcomes and benefits achieved as a result of the agreement.

Collaborative Social Event:

Team-building Event: Organize a social event or team-building activity to celebrate the successful negotiation. This provides an informal setting for participants to bond, relax, and enjoy each other's company outside of the negotiation context.

Public Acknowledgment:

Public Recognition: If appropriate, publicly acknowledge the success of the negotiation through industry awards, recognition programs, or relevant forums. This not only enhances the organization's reputation but also elevates the profile of the individuals involved.

Client Appreciation:

Client Recognition: If the negotiation involves external clients or partners, express appreciation for their trust and collaboration. Consider sending personalized thank-you notes or arranging a small celebration to strengthen the client relationship.

Learning and Growth:

Reflection on Learnings: Take the opportunity to reflect on the lessons learned during the negotiation process. Discuss how the experience has contributed to personal and professional growth, fostering a culture of continuous improvement.

Social Media Acknowledgment:

Digital Recognition: Leverage social media platforms to publicly acknowledge and celebrate the successful negotiation. This allows for broader visibility and recognition within the industry and among peers.

Recognition Awards:

Internal Awards: Establish internal recognition awards specific to successful negotiations. Recognize outstanding contributions, teamwork, or innovative strategies that played a pivotal role in achieving positive outcomes.

Continuing Relationship Building:

Future Collaboration: Use the celebration as an opportunity to discuss and plan for future collaborations. Emphasize the desire to continue building strong relationships and explore additional opportunities for mutual success.

Feedback and Debriefing:

Constructive Feedback: Conduct a debriefing session to gather feedback from all parties involved. This allows for constructive discussions on what worked well, areas for improvement, and insights for future negotiations.

Acknowledgment in Company Communications:

Company-wide Recognition: Integrate the celebration into company-wide communications, newsletters, or internal bulletins. This ensures that the success of the negotiation is acknowledged and celebrated across the entire organization.

Share Success with Stakeholders:

Stakeholder Communication: Communicate the success of the negotiation with relevant stakeholders, such as investors, board members, or regulatory bodies. Keeping stakeholders informed builds trust and confidence in the organization.

Employee Recognition Programs:

Incorporate into Programs: If your organization has employee recognition programs, ensure that the success of the negotiation is incorporated into these initiatives. Recognizing achievements contributes to a positive workplace culture.

Personal Acknowledgment:

Individual Recognition: Personally acknowledge the efforts of individuals who went above and beyond during the negotiation. This can be done through one-on-one meetings, thank-you notes, or informal gatherings.

Showcase Positive Impact:

Impactful Results: Showcase the positive impact of the successful negotiation on the organization, whether it's increased revenue, market share, or improved operational efficiency. This reinforces the value of collaborative efforts.

Continuous Celebration:

Ongoing Recognition: Rather than a one-time event, integrate the celebration into the organization's culture as an ongoing practice. This fosters a mindset of recognizing and celebrating achievements consistently.

Celebrating successful negotiations is not just a formality but a strategic and meaningful practice that reinforces positive relationships, boosts morale, and sets the tone for future collaborations. By acknowledging achievements and expressing gratitude, organizations can cultivate a culture of success, teamwork, and continuous improvement.

Continual Career Development

In the dynamic landscape of today's workforce, continual career development is not just a choice; it's a necessity for staying relevant, motivated, and achieving long-term success. It involves a proactive and intentional approach to acquiring new skills, expanding knowledge, and adapting to the evolving demands of one's profession. Here's a comprehensive guide on the importance of continual career development and effective strategies to navigate the path to professional growth:

Lifelong Learning Mindset:

Embrace a Growth Mindset: Cultivate a mindset that sees challenges as opportunities for learning and growth. Embracing a lifelong learning perspective ensures a continual quest for knowledge and skill enhancement throughout your career.

Self-Assessment and Goal Setting:

Reflect on Your Career: Periodically assess your skills, strengths, and areas for improvement. Set clear and achievable career goals that align with your personal and professional aspirations.

Skill Diversification:

Broaden Your Skill Set: Identify key skills in your industry and beyond. Actively seek opportunities to diversify your skill set, making yourself more adaptable and resilient in the face of industry changes.

Networking and Mentorship:

Build a Professional Network: Regularly engage in networking activities within your industry. Seek out mentors who can offer guidance, share insights, and provide valuable perspectives on your career development journey.

Continuous Education:

Pursue Further Education: Explore formal and informal educational opportunities, such as workshops, webinars, certifications, or advanced degrees. Staying current with industry trends and best practices enhances your professional knowledge.

Stay Informed about Industry Trends:

Monitor Industry Developments: Keep yourself informed about emerging trends, technologies, and changes within your industry. This awareness positions you as a forward-thinking professional and aids in anticipating future skill requirements.

Attend Conferences and Seminars:

Participate in Industry Events: Attend conferences, seminars, and industry events to broaden your perspective, network with professionals, and gain exposure to the latest advancements in your field.

Cross-Functional Experience:

Explore Cross-Functional Roles: Seek opportunities to work on cross-functional projects or take on roles outside your immediate area of expertise. This not only enhances your skill set but also provides a holistic view of organizational dynamics.

Embrace Technology:

Stay Tech-Savvy: Given the rapid evolution of technology, continually update your digital skills. Familiarize yourself with new tools, software, and platforms relevant to your industry.

Professional Development Plans:

Create Personalized Plans: Develop personalized professional development plans that outline specific actions, timelines, and milestones. Regularly review and adjust these plans to ensure they align with your evolving career goals.

Seek Feedback:

Continuous Improvement Feedback: Actively seek feedback from colleagues, supervisors, and mentors. Constructive feedback provides valuable insights into areas where you can improve and grow.

Leadership and Management Training:

Enhance Leadership Skills: If applicable to your career trajectory, invest in leadership and management training. Developing these skills positions you for roles with increased responsibilities and leadership opportunities.

Soft Skills Enhancement:

Focus on Soft Skills: Recognize the importance of soft skills such as communication, emotional intelligence, and adaptability. Continuous refinement of these skills contributes to effective collaboration and leadership.

Build an Online Presence:

Establish Digital Presence: Develop and maintain a professional online presence through platforms like LinkedIn. Share your accomplishments, engage in industry discussions, and connect with professionals in your field.

Time Management and Organization:

Prioritize Time Management: Enhance your time management and organizational skills. Efficiently balancing multiple responsibilities contributes to a productive and fulfilling career.

Join Professional Associations:

Engage in Industry Associations: Become an active member of professional associations related to your field. This involvement provides opportunities for networking, access to resources, and participation in industry discussions.

Side Projects and Entrepreneurial Ventures:

Explore Side Projects: Consider engaging in side projects or entrepreneurial ventures related to your expertise or interests. These endeavors can foster creativity, innovation, and potentially lead to new career opportunities.

Stay Resilient in the Face of Challenges:

Embrace Challenges:*Challenges are inherent in any career journey. Cultivate resilience and view challenges as opportunities to learn, adapt, and strengthen your skills.

Regular Career Check-Ins:

Scheduled Career Reflections: Schedule regular check-ins with yourself to assess your career satisfaction, progress, and alignment with your goals. Adjust your career development strategies as needed.

Pay Attention to Work-Life Balance:

Balance Personal and Professional Life: Strive for a healthy work-life balance. Recognize that personal well-being is integral to professional success and sustainable career development.

Conclusion:

Continual career development is not a one-time endeavor but an ongoing commitment to growth, adaptability, and personal fulfillment. By embracing a mindset of lifelong learning, setting clear goals, and consistently seeking opportunities for improvement, professionals can navigate their careers successfully in an ever-changing landscape. Prioritizing continuous development not only enhances individual capabilities but also contributes to the overall progress of industries and organizations.

THANK YOU FOR READING

Thank you for embarking on the journey of "Mastering Negotiation: A Guide to Elevating Your Career." Your commitment to personal and professional growth is commendable. May the insights within empower you to navigate negotiations with confidence, achieve your aspirations, and continually excel in your career. Happy reading and negotiating!